the year belovèd

sonnets for the seasons of the heart

bobby livingston

copyright statement

Published by TCA (Poetry Publishing),
Glasgow, Scotland.

Cover design & typesetting by TCA.

Cover image by Chris Lawton on Unsplash.

Icons by Flaticon: *Spring Leaves* by Linseed Studios; *Summer Sun* by Freepik; *Autumn Leaves* by Freepik; and *Winter Snowflake* by Vector Stall.

ISBN: 978-0-9571054-6-1

contents

foreword

The Year Belovèd

Love has been written about before. It has been mourned in odes, exalted in sonnets, and questioned in countless forms. Yet it remains inexhaustible—because each heart must learn its own way through joy, longing, and loss. These sixty sonnets are my attempt to trace that journey in full: the cycle of love as it unfolds through the seasons of the heart.

I have leaned into the Shakespearean sonnet not as mimicry, but as homage. Its archaic grammar and formal constraint offer a kind of shelter—a place where emotion can be held, examined, and sometimes transformed. I believe that older English, when spoken with sincerity, still carries the weight and clarity needed to speak of love. It is not outdated—it is enduring.

Each section—Spring, Summer, Autumn, Winter—carries its own mood and movement. The sonnets within them speak of tenderness, desire, grief, and renewal. Some are raw. Some are quiet. All are part of a rhythm I've tried to honour: the way love begins, deepens, falters, and endures.

This book is not a diary, nor a doctrine. It is a gesture—toward completeness, toward complexity, and toward the kind of truth that lovers of every kind might recognize. If you find something here that echoes your own experience, I'll be grateful. If not, I hope the rhythm still carries you somewhere worth remembering.

—bobby livingston

about the author

Bobby Livingston is a poet, writer and bookmaker whose work bridges tradition and personal transformation. Profoundly deaf since late adulthood, he came to poetry as both refuge and revelation—where silence gave rise to rhythm, and loss became lyrical. His sonnets, rooted in Shakespearean cadence and restrained formality, trace the seasons of love with precision, grace, and emotional depth.

Often found walking through Pollok Country Park, his writing is shaped by the turning of the year and the subtle, mythic presence of the Muse. A decorated public speaker and long-time steward of the Glasgow Speakers Club, he has authored books on the craft of oratory, blending eloquence with mentorship. Whether exploring poetic theory or studying French with quiet discipline, he seeks beauty where structure and soul meet.

This collection is a seasonal offering—a reflection of love, language, and the quiet companionship of the Muse.

for the music I'll never hear,
and the Muse who consoles me.

spring

Some say, thy fault is youth, some wantonness;
some say, thy grace is youth and gentle sport…

Sonnet 96—William Shakespeare

—Spring: where love lifts her veil—

In the hush of early bloom, Spring lifts her veil. She is not merely rebirth; she is hunger, revelation, and remembrance. Through archaic verse we journey amidst desire and duty, myth and memory—from the Green Man's whisper in the woods to the sovereign ache of Mary Queen of Scots, lost among the primrose and thistle. Here, womankind is both Muse and Monarch; passion pulses beneath uncertain skies. Let us wander through this budding garden where voices plead, affirm, resist—and where love, like the seasons, turns eternal, ephemeral, and ever unresolved.

—who will believe my verse in time to come—

Hasten man's desire

Buds spring in March to hasten man's desire,
with morning dew, loud calling for his touch;
awake, the earth, her arms of green conspire
to bring his body close in wondrous clutch.
And thou, proud daughter of our planet's womb,
beguile me with thy richness of intent;
thy form, a beauty born to stave off gloom,
and maketh mine own heart full well content.
Sweet spring, that minstrel season of the bard,
seduces hearts, it begs them to want more,
and thou and I, as fate doth kindly guard,
are blessed by fleeting joys we both adore.
Thus let our love reflect the turning year
and find in every season love sincere.

—in every season love sincere—

The Green Man e'er ordains

Last year I yearned for thee when love was green,
unready to receive my heart's request;
now April's gentle hand, with blooms serene,
hath bidden slumbered buds to manifest.
Thus, nature's hand doth guide each tender heart,
unseen, yet felt, her whispers stir the air;
her mystic touch doth bid love's buds to start,
unfolding virgin leaves with endless care.
Now zephyrs kiss the bloom with breath so sweet,
love stirs unbidden, shy, yet growing strong;
in verdant meadows earth and heaven meet,
as hearts unseen, sing nature's ageless song:
Sap flows to leaves as love flows through our veins,
this sacred rite the Green Man e'er ordains.

—now zephyrs kiss the bloom with breath so sweet—

Man of Will

Fall not upon the salty spear of love
nor sup the poisoned chalice of false hearts,
thy 'Man of Dreams' is chosen from above
but comes to thee in pauses, fits and starts.
To seek is not to find but chase one's tail
—the laws are written, and it must be so:
to search is not to find but set coarse sail
and travel across oceans full of woe.
Love comes in truly unexpected ways,
like apples fall in unsuspecting laps;
be open to its magic all thy days
or caught within its dead-ends and its traps.
To thee then comes the truest 'Man of Will';
thy purpose to secure, thy heart to still.

—be open to its magic all thy days—

To doubt is women's way

Why hast thou low regard unto thyself
when beauty blossoms from thy very core;
self-criticism undermines by stealth,
beseech I thee its poison to ignore.
No flower blooms that first was not a seed
nor apple gathered sate 'til it be ripe;
thou art sweet fruit, pure woman to thy creed
with seasons in thy heart and tears to wipe.
To doubt but of oneself is women's way,
thy gentle soul doth lead it so to be
but I thy noble prince shall demons slay
that thou might smile and life may set thee free:
A man must love the garden that he sows
else weeds will strangle out his darling rose.

—nor apple gathered sate 'til it be ripe—

Lament for Mary Stuart

Now Nature hangs her mantle green full brave,
and larks do lift their songs above the lea;
but she lies bound beneath the silent grave,
where love and light are but a memory.
She was the Queen of gallant France ere long,
with roses twyned in hair so blythe and free;
yet traitor winds blew cold through Tyne's sad song,
and stilled the harp of realms yoked by the sea.
Her love was lost, her joy was fled awa';
the daisy blooms, yet she in bondage dwelled,
with none to hear her song, nor heed her law,
save ghosts that whispered through yon ancient cell.
O Spring! thou mock'st her with thy scented breath
—for freedom's kiss, she'd trade thy bloom for death.

—where love and light are but a memory—

Womankind

Canst thou not love as love was thine to give,
hold back the sea's advance without regret;
know thou art art and art's desire to love
unearths deep roots the world to upset?
Invisible, man's norms do thee control;
'Do as I say,' his tenor shapes thy path
and carves for thee a burden thou must thole
—experiencing thus thy fair earned wrath!
Attune thine ear to seasons of the heart
and question not the greatness of its gift,
each loving stitch thy pattern doth impart
as man's controlling whims are cast adrift.
Love is the rod and staff which doth unbind;
the force which frees the heart of womankind.

—attune thine ear to seasons of the heart—

Dark be thy mask

Behind thy lacéd veil art thou content
to forsake the true nature of thy heart?
Dark be thy mask yet darker love's lament
when woman from her path seeks to depart.
Yield not to false demands that lead astray
nor cede thy plight to calls whose aims mislead;
through thee tradition wafteth its bouquet
that man may love and woman be his lead.
Thus, to thy sex, and it alone, be true;
proud woman like a flower blooms in June,
her gentle way the work she's born to do,
to love, to serve, to dance and sing in tune.
Thy lacéd veil conceals complaisant ways
and man is lured to love thee all his days.

—thus, to thy sex, and it alone, be true—

Acceptest thou my pleas?

To thee I write these words in purest praise,
unfettered testament of heart's desire;
to be beloved by thee, my soul still prays,
a love that bids thou dost my heart inspire.
And when inspired this quill doth rouse a flame,
exotic 'tis to laud thy worldly charm;
no steeple mountain high my verse to tame,
nor grammar doth its rhythmic flow alarm.
Yet, far across the ocean thou dost dwell,
thy visage near in dreams, afar in truth;
my plaintive heart doth beg thy love's sweet spell
to nurture verse and bloom poetic youth:
Words flow when thou acceptest still my pleas;
words, tsunami amidst emotive seas.

—words, tsunami amidst emotive seas—

Sonnet for a distant love

Across the seven seas my beauty lies,
the pillow, downy soft, her curls to meet;
enveloped by her dreams and longing sighs,
her tide of love shall all distance defeat.
And I, drawn west to east by faith of heart,
bear tempests as a sovereign doth his pride,
discouraged not by failure nor false start
to navigate my pleasure by her side.
Love knoweth only how to breathe desire
betwixt a man and woman of good will;
to seek, to need, to want is passion's fire
—it holds us tight but never leaves us still.
To thee my love I offer up my soul
that we may merge and make this world whole.

—love knoweth only how to breathe desire—

Tell thy story unto me

O Mother Earth from whose womb I was born,
grieve not that mine own purpose be untrue;
for through thy seed of hope my heart's adorn'd,
my words and verse fair tribute unto you.
Thy bosom rich with stories yet untold,
like proud magnetic north holds one enthralled;
my duty clear, to listen not to scold,
thy precious gift fore'er must be recalled.
O Mystery within, reveal thy soul!
And hide it not from mankind's blinkered eye
that he may live in truth and e'er console
those blind to love-kissed stories ne'er to die.
Fair beauty tell thy story unto me
and words and love fore'er will set man free.

—thy bosom rich with stories yet untold—

Thou art treasure for my quill

Is there a truer resonance than thine
inspiring deep poetic thoughts of love,
a stronger bond connecting the divine
from heart to heart to honour thee above?
My woman! Thou art treasure for my quill,
a well of inky magic to unleash
wild symphonies of words designed to thrill
my humble soul to scribe and say its piece.
Hide not behind the silky veil of night
nor vanish to thy Muse-like Realm on high,
abandon not my prose without fierce fight
but make each verse a vow to thee for aye!
The marriage of our spirits was foretold;
to honour thee I'll write these words in gold.

—hide not behind the silky veil of night—

The lass o' my dreams…

Speed Bonnie Boat to the lass o' my dreams
o'er foamy waters and into her arms;
onwards to beauty anointed by queens
who know of her love, its depth and its charms.
Loud the winds howl as the bow cuts its course,
close to the stream of my heart's true desire,
steering its path in a bold tour de force
while sails sing sweet like a heavenly choir.
Burned are the hopes of lovers unwilling
to act as their hearts command them to do;
make haste, else fear a life unforgiving
where love knows thy name but 'tis not for you:
Lass, I shall come with the bravest of hearts
defeating wild waves, their fits and their starts.

—onwards to beauty anointed by queens—

Three little words…

Three words come but as strangers to thy lips
when I, besotted by thy beauty, dare
to ask; they sit unheard as sailing ships
do sit on silent seas bereft of air.
How simple yet how touching words can be
when from the heart they emanate in truth;
their riddle is a timeless mystery
that calls upon love's valour and its couth.
A constellation lives within thy heart,
its shyness fills my galaxy's unease
but truth will out—its flow of verse to start,
a Melody for souls on bended knees:
Three little words will make my dreams come true,
when from thy lips I hear an 'I love you'.

—how simple yet how touching words can be—

My Muse

My Muse sits high upon her queenly throne
to cast her eye over my heartfelt prose;
her joy-inspiring love's for me alone,
it nurtures me through miseries and woes.
Her beauty is the gift within her heart,
long hair and heaving breasts do not compare,
her touch, pure electricity to start
this flow of words which come to me through air.
O Muse, forgive the passions of my soul,
the torment and desires I express thus,
my outpourings, my dreams to make us whole
until we blend into one single us.
My Muse, reach out to grasp my poet hand,
craft these fine words which lovers understand.

—her touch, pure electricity to start—

Vernal awakening?

When spring imbues thy form with vernal grace
and silvered dew ascends to kiss its bloom,
thy Sylvan Breast shall yield to love's embrace
whilst root and tendril weave their verdant room.
And if, perchance, love's seed doth take its keep,
as boughs entwine to crown thee fair and bright,
my dreams shall wend where passion's roots run deep
to bathe thee in the dawn's resplendent light.
Yet, fleeting though love's bloom may seem to be,
it gathers strength as sun doth rise on high;
the ember swells to flame in ecstasy
and bids our hearts, unbound, to touch the sky.
But shall we, tempted thus, by summer, soar
or falter 'fore love's warmth opens the door?

—and if, perchance, love's seed doth take its keep—

summer

Then happy I, that love and am beloved
where I may not remove nor be removed.

Sonnet 25—William Shakespeare

—Summer: where love is sung and tested—

Summer serenades the soul with golden fire. In language steeped in longing and lore, we journey amidst passion's bloom and longing's ache—from whispered kisses beneath crimson skies to the bold declarations of love's old dance. Here, desire is both playful and profound, a force that binds and bewilders. The Mistress, the Muse, the Wife—each figure casts her spell, shaping man's heart with beauty, wisdom, and truth. Beneath the sun's embrace, we explore fidelity, temptation, and the fruit of life itself. Come, step into this season of fullness, where love is sung, tested, and transformed—and where the heat of longing gives rise to the legacy of devotion.

—summer's lease hath all too short a date—

Summer's gold

Thy beauty dawns as doth the summer's gold,
to warm man's heart and savage ire allay;
thy locks, like burnished chestnut, rich, unrolled,
thy tender smile bids roughest breast obey.
By Heaven's hand anointed, thee I know,
thy love the honey'd nectar none surpass;
a balm divine, no soul may e'er forego
with sculpted grace to match thy spirit's glass.
Thy touch I crave, thy hand to soothe my woe,
thy fingers light upon my furrow'd brow;
thy voice, like whispered winds, shall gently blow,
thy touch alone my storm-toss'd soul allow.
When morn's fair sun doth gild thy peerless mien,
my wayward heart finds peace in thee, my queen.

—thy tender smile bids roughest breast obey—

Timeless sighs

Beneath the sun's embrace, thy warmth doth glow,
as fragrant zephyrs whisper through the air;
thy laughter, like the blossoms' tender show,
unfoldeth worlds of beauty, rich and rare.
These golden rays that dance upon thy skin
are tapestry of light and shadow spun;
thy gaze doth spark, where passions deep begin,
my summer fire that rivals e'en the sun.
Yet time, though bold, this fire shall ne'er consume
for summer's essence liveth in thine eyes;
thy radiance, love's greatest ever tune,
a melody embracing timeless sighs.
To hold thee 'neath the sun and ne'er regret,
is love eternal, 'yond the seasons set.

—summer's essence liveth in thine eyes—

A stolen kiss

Tonight, when sun 'neath crimson sky doth set
and whispers stray where zephyr'd breezes play;
our hearts, unspoken, shall their bonds be met,
as stolen lips ignite the fading day?
And will this moment linger in the air,
as lips, erst strangers, softly intertwine;
the rush of passion silencing despair,
as yearning souls with oaths unspoke align?
This night surrounds us, velvet-soft and deep
and starlight weaveth webs 'cross boundless skies;
the world retreats, and in this love we keep,
a universe unfolding with our sighs.
Through stolen moments, love's sweet truth is shown
and summer's warmth will claim us as its own.

—a universe unfolding with our sighs—

Love's old dance

Beguile me with thine eyes and never cease
to love me as my love may still be thine;
rouse me with thy looks, interrupt my peace
—of thee to be adored is hope divine!
Thy gaze upon my visage here today
gives insight to the beauty of thy soul.
O come, my love, and promise thou shalt stay;
abide within my heart and make me whole.
To stroke the gentle contours of thy cheek,
to dream of kisses passionate and true,
to want and want again until I'm weak
—my all-consuming thoughts are aye of you.
Thine eyes art wondrous agents of romance,
enthral me with their charm through love's old dance.

—to dream of kisses passionate and true—

Only love

O she, who in her innocence persuades
man's heart to flutter at her very sight,
afeard of naught her beauty ne'er evades
attentive eyes upon her graceful flight.
How could such beauty pass without due praise
or go unnoticed through man's daily grind;
alone, she is the one for whom he prays,
the woman of his dreams, one of a kind.
But glamour being skin deep is just a lure
to catch man's weaknesses for all to see;
he falls for curvy hips with thoughts impure
when what he needs is love to set him free.
Each woman holds her beauty for man's eye
but only love can e'er him satisfy.

—the woman of his dreams, one of a kind—

True fidelity

Engulféd heart of mine deceive me not:
Is true love cruel, or cruel that she be kind?
Hath she her pride, no price may she be bought,
elusive as a summer breeze, and blind?
Can bitter pain be life's only pleasure
but ne'er be love's firm conquest or delight?
Is love for fools to repent at leisure?
No rosy bed for Cupid's pupil's plight?
Unseat me of my manhood if 'tis so!
Rage, my blood, rage and ne'er tire of raging
for beauty in mine arms I'll ne'er forego
till my bod is frail and gript through ageing.
Damned, I shall fight, though damned I shall not be:
my love, true fidelity, is with thee.

—no rosy bed for Cupid's pupil's plight—

The chosen one

My lady glides on heels afore mine eyes,
a poem made of curves to match her rhyme;
such elegance doth make my pulse to rise
and maketh my brain flee the woes of time.
Each step she takes brings music to mine ears,
a shiver down my spine that I could be
the man to hold her close throughout the years
or fated be the hand that sets her free.
This is the truth that e'er befalls mankind:
to love until love hurts when least it should,
to seek out beauty's pleasure for the mind
yet know the Gods of grace oft one exclude.
Through love, this fleeting moment, hath allowed
my feet to dance with hers amongst the crowd.

—a poem made of curves to match her rhyme—

A worldly whole

Thine eloquence is music to mine ears,
a symphony of sonnets set to please;
a silky balm applied throughout the years,
like crêpe Georgette or kisses sent to tease.
Art thou a dreamy château of my mind,
a mystery in lemon soufflé curls?
A pot-pourri of lover's thoughts entwined,
embracing Java coffee frothed to whorls?
O love, the finest treasure to be found
behind each spectral veil of morning light
are syllables upon thy lips formed round
and vowels from thy heart to hold me tight.
Come, spread the word wise wisdom of thy soul
to form this man into a worldly whole.

—thine eloquence is music to mine ears—

Fruit of life

Into thy heart I delve to find my way
when rivers dry and seasons seek no joy;
frustration marks the start of every day
until, my love, thou dost devise thy ploy.
How barren life can be without thy grace,
grey skies and clouds do follow me around;
no hope beyond the brightness of thy face,
though through thine eyes true love doth yet abound.
One smile is all it takes, a gentle touch,
to mend anew my world of loveless waste,
a silent stratagem that says so much
when lips on lips thy love is all I taste.
'Tis thou who giveth me the fruit of life;
'tis I who beg thee now to be my wife.

—how barren life can be without thy grace—

All for one and one for all

Three loves have I, and each doth shape my soul,
not fleeting whims nor passion's empty call,
but artistry, devotion, and control
—a triad bound where love doth rule them all.
The Muse ignites, where wildest dreams take flight,
the Mistress frees, where longing dares to be,
the wife consoles, where steadfast love burns bright
—thus heart and mind must weave this tapestry.
For love is not a single thread entwined,
but cords that twist in harmony and grace;
it bends to passion, reason, and the mind,
and finds its truth where all three loves embrace.
Yet one alone doth prove my heart in test
—the greatest love is thou; thou art the best.

—for love is not a single thread entwined—

Thou art more than fleshy form

O Mistress, cleavage-deep, mine eyes to please,
delight me with the splendours of thy breast;
to fall for thee I do with willing ease:
'Sweet maiden of my dreams', thou art the best!
Thy curves were sculpted by a loving hand,
the mason of creation formed thee well,
shaping thy bosom boldly here to stand
like luscious fruit, whereon mine eyes do dwell.
But Mistress, thou art more than fleshy form,
a corset filled to spark my heart's desire;
through thee my words emerge and then reform
into these sonnets which thou dost inspire.
Thou art my Muse, my beauty and delight,
my one true love, the reason why I write.

—the mason of creation formed thee well—

I shall play thy harp

To place this crimson rose upon thy breast,
sweet summer dew, its taste upon my tongue;
To search thy comely form from east to west,
still yearning for fresh pleasures of the young;
To crave the secret candour of thy touch,
soft strokes, betwixt these silken sheets of shame;
To seek thy lusting moans of double Dutch,
and know my love for thee shall never tame;
These passions forge my fate to set me free,
yet hidden must they burn 'neath virtue's guise;
the world shall never learn my thirst for thee,
nor glimpse the sinful longing in thine eyes.
O Mistress! Sing to me thy summer song
and I shall play thy harp this whole night long.

—to crave the secret candour of thy touch—

The language of the night

This kiss shall rend the silence of our night,
all words betwixt us now remain unsaid;
unspoken thoughts in fervent bonds unite
—lust's sovereign will doth rule each yearning head.
Our bodies, thus obliging, lose command,
submissive hearts to nature's voice give ear;
a passion binds us fast at fate's demand
and leads us to our climax—sweet yet drear.
The tongue of night is breath both hushed and deep,
a mystery enshrouded in its spell;
it endeth surely in love's deathly keep,
the cruellest woe of heaven and of hell.
This night hath neither shadow nor a tongue,
yet speaketh through the flames in bosoms sprung.

—this night hath neither shadow nor a tongue—

Dost thou blush?

I shall upon thy breast lay willing tongue
whilst thou dost yield to milk the morning dew;
forsooth, my guilty pleasures lie among
these mad desires that others find taboo.
Thou art my queen in wild, obliging ways,
thy bod is blest release for manly whim;
to scribe for thee adds purpose to my days
and cravings deep for pleasures thou dost brim!
O Mistress, dost thou blush to learn 'tis so,
that I enrapt by thee am spellbound held?
Or hast thou pride in knowing I'm thy Beau
and wantonness to make our bodies meld?
Enwrap me in the beauty of thy trust;
accept me as I am—A Man of Lust!

—thou art my queen in wild, obliging ways—

'twas all my wealth

When through our love I gave to thee my seed
and summer blossomed ripe upon the branch,
thy fruit was all my sustenance and need,
a platter served to nourish pure romance.
Warm shafts of sun did beat upon our backs,
new love was seasoned by its sunny rays,
it led us to enjoy love's fulsome tracks:
these were our treasured moments, special days!
My seed was all I had, 'twas all my wealth,
thou cherished it and makest it to grow,
then blessed it with the goodness of thy health
and bore it forth for all the world to show.
Our love was warmly cherished 'neath the sun,
it brought us close and begot us our son.

—my seed was all I had, 'twas all my wealth—

autumn

That time of year thou mayst in me behold
when yellow leaves, or none, or few do hang…

Sonnet 73—William Shakespeare

—Autumn: love's endurance amid decay—

Autumn arrives not with thunder, but with hush. In this season of fading light and falling leaves, you are invited into a realm of memory, longing, and quiet transformation. Through sonnets steeped in reverie, we witness love's endurance amid decay, and hope's flicker in the shadow of time. The Muse is both companion and compass—guiding the heart through sorrow, courage, and the sacred ache of devotion. Each verse is a leaf turned, revealing the beauty of what was and the truth of what remains. Let us walk gently through this golden dusk, where love is tested, remembered, and reborn—and where the soul, like the season, prepares to let go, yet never forget.

—for thy sweet love remember'd such wealth brings—

Did I offend in summer's loving arms?

Bold autumn turning rich green, amber-brown,
wild winds exposing wiry veins on leaves,
as chestnuts fall, the season wears its frown;
cruel calling card of winter ne'er deceives.
October's veil doth slip, as slip it must,
exposing earth's eternal story true:
revolving globe of hope in which we trust,
shedding its snakelike skin to aye renew.
O beauty of this land, why must thou flee?
Did I offend in summer's loving arms?
And hath thine ire ris'n thus to smite mine e'e
and makest thou me blind to nature's charms?
Of this I shall resist until I die,
for autumn's golden beauty's in mine eye.

—o beauty of this land, why must thou flee—

Regal emblem

Dark purple, regal emblem of the heart,
rich autumn hue where sun sets o'er the hill;
sharp be its lacquered nails, their touch to start
this homage to old ways that holds us still.
No words define the nature of our pact,
'tis ancient as the trees and written so;
we are but players for this season's act,
mute agents to the laws of fortune's flow.
To thee I offer love, this love is thine,
a rosy apple hanging on the bough,
and wish upon a star as souls entwine
and call thy name aloud and wonder how.
Love knoweth ways mere mortals dare to fear;
unbidden flames erupt in hearty cheer.

—we are but players for this season's act—

I searched for thee

Love hath her cards played wisely for my heart,
no fickle fortune's breeze may dim desire;
love's wish was wisdom's pleasure from the start
—a solemn vow to kindle passion's fire.
Now maiden fair holds tightly to my chest,
her days of longing gladly are they o'er;
true faithfulness she held within her breast
to crown me as her king and love me more.
Tell me this is no dream of fancy flight,
that love, at last, endows me with her charms,
that torment may no longer rule each night
but be dissolved between her loving arms?
Love, how I sought thee oft but ne'er thee found,
'til thee thyself decided I be crowned.

—love's wish was wisdom's pleasure from the start—

On seeking true love

Why must the sun go down to end each day
and darkness hide thy beauty from mine eyes;
doth truth reveal, as seasons fade away,
that love itself can never compromise?
To know thee without touch or sight or sound
yet feel thee, deep-embedded in my heart;
to spend each day in restless 'lost and found'
then learn in finding thee that love is art.
This is my hell, the weakness of my soul,
to crave thy fruit yet never must I taste;
to search for thee, my never-ending goal,
a goal that cuts me deep with futile waste.
O love, thy wondrous art is wholesome truth,
yet I, thy humble servant, ne'er it soothe.

—this is my hell, the weakness of my soul—

Duende

Whither dost thou go to dance duende,
lost on the strings of a Spanish guitar,
think'st thou of me and my love so empty,
abandoned, alone on this shore afar?
Swirl thou thy pleats and thy polka-dot hips,
tapping thy toes to the zeal of the dance,
hastening our love with fire on thy lips
and memories deep—of our wild romance?
Lost in the night, where love knows no ending
yet trapped by headwinds that blew us apart;
flow with thy heart which knows no pretending,
steeped in tradition, deep love and pure art.
Music and dance will hold us together
—but love is the bond that lasts forever.

—love is the bond that lasts forever—

Each willing heart

When Cupid's arrow maimed us to defeat,
knowing fate had cast our suffering state,
my sullen eyes reflected there to meet
thy pale visage, bereft of love's estate.
How could mythical law accede to this
—two souls kept worlds apart but never still,
two wounded hearts, their kisses e'er to miss,
with passions doused anew by autumn's chill?
Resent I not the fate that wrought us pain,
yet grieve the hours love's warmth was cast away;
no hand may hold our hearts in cold disdain,
for passion's fire defies the fading day:
It bends the rules to meet each willing heart,
unbinding ancient mores, true love to start.

—passion's fire defies the fading day—

Let our hearts be still

Thy soft regard doth lift my longing heart,
to it I turn, when eyes fall closed at night
and in the sweetest dreams thou ne'er dost part
but love me long until the morning light.
No chasm deep nor ocean may divide
nor endless space defeat our kindred souls;
the universal law of love decides,
we are but agents under its control.
O foolish be the ones who sacrifice
each living day without true love's consent;
are they prepared to pay the highest price,
to be unloved—and never thus resent?
Love's deep and wondrous hand defines our will;
come love me love and let our hearts be still.

—the universal law of love decides—

Time's travesty

Rejoice sweet Muse! My work is nature's salt,
pure season to thy beauty's majesty;
thee I adore bereft of pleasure's fault
but wilfully reproach time's travesty.
Upon Greek's lyric pedestal, sit thou,
eternal goddess of the mystic lore,
whilst I, mere mortal, draw my poet's plough
to toil for thee 'til toil I can no more.
Muse, thou art blest, untouched by autumn's hand,
unchanging as the stars that crown the night;
yet I, who toil, am bound by time's command
to strive to honour thee with all my might.
And so, in earnest strife I pen for thee,
that through my words thy grace shall set me free.

—upon Greek's lyric pedestal, sit thou—

When courage fails

The heart disowns the brain when courage fails,
to make man weak before love's douce request;
his passion, now defeated, turns and pales
leaving him naught but regrets to digest.
How foolish, then, to follow not one's heart,
when it, the centre of man's soul, commands;
hath reason fought to overturn love's cart,
and leave man now to question where he stands.
The heart is wisdom's true and guiding light,
fear not the path it sets, though blind thee be;
it leads man through the darkness of each night
to find true love—a love that sets him free.
When courage fails, the heart disowns the brain,
let not its feeble voice be love's refrain.

—how foolish, then, to follow not one's heart—

Reach me from beyond

To dream that dreams be true, and night be day
and day itself an everlasting joy,
where love, supping her finest wine, would say,
'I'll be thy maid if thou wilt be my boy'.
My heart, residing thus above yon cloud,
floating on slipstreams glorious to see,
inspired to sing and raise my voice aloud
to say, 'I love and love but only thee'.
Yet dreams are merely fantasies of whim
deceiving thus the fragile ghosts of night,
who wake amidst the chill of morning grim,
though ne'er can lose thy beauty from their sight.
Hold out thy hand to reach me from beyond,
for love, my love for thee, shall aye respond.

—yet dreams are merely fantasies of whim—

Goodbye?

When from thy lips I sensed the word 'goodbye,'
and felt its blade cut deep into my chest,
all hope evaporated in a sigh;
Lord knows I've yearned for thee—but love knows best.
This thought of parting held me in a trance,
unspoken though it was, mine eyes did blur.
Once love had held us close in merry dance,
now chest to breast, our hearts, do they concur?
And then, thy lips bestowed on me a kiss,
and from their touch, all worries were put right.
To me, thou art the one—my favourite Miss,
the lass I'll ne'er forgo without a fight.
So deep in love, my senses oft confuse,
but then thou set'st me right, my darling Muse.

—and then, thy lips bestowed on me a kiss—

The fog upon thy pillow

When through thy love I feel the greatest need,
a longing that unquenched dries out my soul,
I turn to memories, my heart to feed,
for truth, 'tis they alone that make me whole.
Thine eyes reveal our story of long past,
when we held hands and dreamt of what could be,
the future that we hoped was ours to last,
a love divine and deeper than the sea.
But fortune laid thee low once we were wed;
the fog upon thy pillow rarely lifts.
For thee my heart hath strained, till it hath bled,
and lo, to God I prayed: return thy gifts!
O love, the greatest blessing was we met;
of this I hold most dear, without regret.

—when we held hands and dreamt of what could be—

When thou art gone

When thou art gone, my world turns palest blue;
no mortal soul compares to thee, my love.
Though empires wane and tides no more renew,
thou dost remain, a gift from realms above.
This distance lingers, stealing light away,
a lost horizon, shrouded in the mist.
The seasons fade to spectres dull and grey,
though I, forlorn, in yearning still persist.
I beg for thee—to soothe this aching woe,
to whisper soft, thy voice my soul doth crave.
Forgive this heart that doth its torment show,
for love must speak, ere death our souls enslave.
Thou turnst me inside-out, then out once more,
bereft of thee, what refuge lies in store?

—the seasons fade to spectres dull and grey—

Each woman plays her part

True love, I searched for thee but never found
longevity's caress or hopeful kiss,
bereft of these two sisters and their sound
my only pleasure was to reminisce.
My Mistress held thy secret close to heart,
deep-hidden, 'neath her guarded, tender breast,
but secrets cause a wedge to force apart
each vow of love, as Cupid doth attest.
No longer do I seek thy holy grail;
perfection is a dream without an end,
it scars all happiness and makes life pale,
each loyal follower doth it offend.
Love grows from heart to heart in unchained grace,
each woman plays her part through warm embrace.

—no longer do I seek thy holy grail—

I beg thee in me live

I hope I dwell, that hope may dwell in me:
my dreams undone by fate's unfettered fist,
its savage blow hath made me blind to see
the love one finds in keeping Muse's tryst.
Her guiding hand leads me into the light
of realms unknown where daybreak glimmers through;
my heart rejoiceth at her sacred sight,
once hope was gone, but O how hope is true!
Afeard, she hid, concealed from prying eyes,
yet deep within my breast she aye remained,
for hope's a stalwart truth that never dies,
a beauty that fore'er remains unchained.
So hope, once more in me, I beg thee live
that Lady Muse may guide and always give.

—her guiding hand leads me into the light—

winter

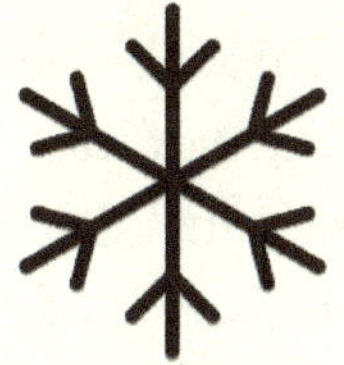

How like a winter hath my absence been
from thee, the pleasure of the fleeting year!

Sonnet 97—William Shakespeare

—Winter: where silence holds the ache—

Winter does not ask permission—it arrives with frost upon the soul and silence upon the tongue. In this season of reckoning, we walk through shadows cast by memory, loss, and the quiet defiance of love. These sonnets do not mourn alone; they rise against the chill, bearing witness to grief's weight and the resilience of the heart. Here, love is tested not by time, but by absence, silence, and fate's cruel hand. Yet even in the coldest night, the Muse endures—her ink a flame, her verse a refuge. Let us enter this solstice with courage, where truth is not buried but bared, and where the soul, like the land, lies fallow only to rise again.

—in black ink my love may still shine bright—

The darkest night

So desolate, the landscape of my mind,
a bleak, foreboding field where love once stood;
sad memories of life do e'er rewind
a death that broke my heart and did no good.
Those bitter tears I shed, how deep they cut,
as I so longed for precious days of past
where laughter's sprightly legs did proudly strut
'cross golden fields of hope once unsurpassed.
O joy, thou fleeting ghost! come once again,
for misery's a burden much to bear
and broken though I was my life regained
new wings to soar into thy loving care.
O loss thou scarred my soul without a fight
but love—thou led'st me through the darkest night.

—o joy, thou fleeting ghost! come once again—

Love beyond time

Beneath the soil I hope one day to meet,
in calm repose, thy love I knew in life;
thy warm embrace, once more, my soul to greet
in endless unity against all strife.
Thy loss cut deeper than a mighty sword
when love was at the apex of its flight;
O how I cried and blasphemed 'gainst the Lord
who cruelly snatched thy beauty from my sight.
But love, I've come in time to understand,
resides within the spiritual domain;
our bodies fade into life's dusty sand
till only spectral silence doth remain.
Though separate in physics and in time
our souls blend to love's reason and its rhyme.

—our bodies fade into life's dusty sand—

Is love not love?

Is love not love when distance holds the cards
or time divides earth's morning from its night?
Must we, like fleeting ships on fractured shards,
be lost and cast adrift without a fight?
Am I to ache until I ache no more,
to feel but ether's distance on a whim;
to hold my breath until my lungs are sore
then learn how love with thee doth wax but slim?
Fate hath decreed that thou and I are two,
divided thus, yet never truly one,
denied our sup of lovers' special brew,
though what the flesh doth lose, the soul hath won!
I'll know thee in my heart and always crave;
my love, I'll sleep with thee beyond the grave.

—am I to ache until I ache no more—

A heart adrift

I love thee as the poet's lines art styled,
I care for thee when others fail the test;
thou cravest darkness to be free and wild,
then treatest me the way thou dost the rest.
False hope thou givest, proclaiming thy need,
in wanton wiles seducing with thine eyes;
my love, I am but one, as we agreed,
though, Lord, I tire of sharing—hear my sighs!
Thy heart doth scatter wide its store, I know,
it spreads its love like wishes on the wind,
revelling in its pleasures as they grow,
yet leaving me to feel as though I sinned.
For thee I try, but love doth pierce my heart;
'tis best for all—agree we must—to part.

—my love, I am but one, as we agreed—

Frost upon my soul

My cruelest love, thou art a butterfly
who drinketh nectar from the widest shore,
wild stamens ne'er thy taste shall satisfy
whilst thou wert made to hunger yet for more.
Ephemeral—thy wings reach out to touch
new love where'er thy restless heart doth stray;
to need and need again and want so much
love's lusty fuel to brighten up thy day.
Thy wings, brushing my heart, do always sting,
their airy touch leaves frost upon my soul:
for love that cannot root nor blossoms bring,
knows neither summer's warmth nor spring's control.
Thy fleeting soul leaves shadows on my heart
and fragile flames that die—then fall apart.

—thy wings, brushing my heart, do always sting—

A veil of silence

Now silence weaves its spell upon thy tongue,
thy lips be locked for reasons none can say;
why hast thou plunged my heart ‘mongst sorrow’s throng
where love’s true voice ne’er finds a home to stay?
Those years, where in thy garden I did tend,
count they for naught upon thy heart today?
The harvest of thy heart doth come to end
on fears unsaid, false fears thy love betray.
No love deserves a man who will not hear,
though I be deaf thy conscience e’er was known;
its gentle grace beguiled me year by year
—why hast thou now my steadfast love outgrown?
Though silence doth our hearts in shadows keep,
yet love, unspoken, wakes where none dare sleep.

—though I be deaf thy conscience e’er was known—

Frosted silence

Upon the morrow, frost doth veil the ground,
a spectral shroud o'er fields of barren white;
yet in my hand, a missive, love profound,
doth venture forth into the chilling night.
Thou hast but silence as thy sole reply,
the frigid winds thy sent affection steal;
each whispered vow doth fade beneath the sky,
a love unmarked, thy heart shall ne'er reveal.
Yet, spite thy scorn, my quill shall not refrain;
its ardent ink on parchment doth bestow
a verse immortal, born from love's disdain,
to warm my heart where winter's winds still blow.
Though love denied, my verse shall yet endure;
its fire doth blaze, eternal and most pure.

—thou hast but silence as thy sole reply—

O Muse, my eternal refuge

In silent torment, love stood by my side
with secret vows my pain to be defied;
raw aches and curses wrestling to subside,
where sound once lived, now poetry is plied.
True words I scribe as tears well in mine eyes;
no maid of mortal birth conceived is she,
where once a void would register deep sighs,
now ink across each parchment flows for thee.
O Muse! thy love doth express through my quill
deep gratitude, that thou shouldst salve my wound
and by thy gift, my soul dost find its will
to frame each page with love my heart consumed.
Through thee, O Muse, I rise 'bove mortal bounds;
thy love my soul enshrines where purpose sounds.

—with secret vows my pain to be defied—

Thou art dust

O thou, who wield'st the ever-turning wheel,
a tyrant bound by threads of wayward chance;
thy tempest beats upon my brow with zeal,
yet I shall rise and meet thee in thy dance.
No more shall fortune mock my humbled frame
nor cast me as a pawn in cruel design,
for though thou bear'st the weight of worldly fame,
thy hollow grasp shall never shadow mine.
Thy fickle wrath may darken youth's fair bloom,
yet love and valour shake thee from thy throne;
I curse thee not, nor tremble at my doom,
for fate is naught when strength is but mine own.
I am the wind that stirs the raging sea
and thou art dust that dare contend with me.

—no more shall fortune mock my humbled frame—

My life of fateful shadows

Life is dancing shadows from a lantern,
a flimsy stage for men who act as fools;
playing out their lives like spoiled children
whilst fate concocts a drama O so cruel.
To rise, to fight, to fall—yet know not when,
to do no good yet feign'st to be a saint;
deception rules the hearts of shallow men,
mere sheep upon the path fate's hand doth paint.
O Goodness, prick the canvas of man's soul!
And lead him not into his darkest night
but lead him forth by truth and wise counsel,
for wrongs run deep yet love re-sets them right.
Love lights the stage where mankind plays his part,
redeeming every soul and wayward heart.

—deception rules the hearts of shallow men—

I warm myself in thee

A log upon the fire to chase the chill,
soft kisses linger on thy lips so sweet;
thou art my Queen, more mine than Heaven's will,
for in thy presence, I fall at thy feet!
How hast thou rendered me a ruin'd wreck,
besotted as I am by thy dark eyes:
O! Full my soul doth plead to graze thy neck
and lose myself in thawing endless sighs.
Thy beauty oft doth stir mine ardent ways
on nights when winter's cold stops by my door,
but love, I'll love thee true for all my days,
for loving thee stands writ in passion's store.
I warm myself in thee this solstice night
for ice itself would melt upon thy sight.

—but love, I'll love thee true for all my days—

Let's love this coldest night

Lie naked as the yuletide snow, my love,
soft contours on the field before mine eyes;
envelop all the earth, as God above,
who forms within my heart the deepest sighs.
To thee, mine eyes are drawn this shortest day
when sun is low and ice forms on my breath;
behold I thee with mortal thoughts that say,
"Though love be short, I'll love thee unto death."
Now yule casts wide its frosty petticoat,
while sun and shadow wage their fading fight,
that thou and I may love as fate doth tote
to blend our lips through darkness into light.
Love warms herself by acts that touch the heart;
come love this coldest night and never part.

—to thee, mine eyes are drawn this shortest day—

What once was ours

Thy memory abides and never wanes;
in light and shadow still thy graces glow,
as I, thy faithful suitor, sought the chains
that bound our love in patterns none could know.
'Twas I who held thee tightly in mine arms
and kissed thy ruby lips till dawn broke free;
thou softly filled my heart with all thy charms
and all I was, was thine—and thine to be.
Thy treasures flowed but I, through pride did stray,
I searched too deep for what could not be found;
was I too grave, too formal in my way
or did some jest turn all thy love to ground?
Would time's return restore what once was ours
or break again what bloomed 'neath gentler hours?

—I searched too deep for what could not be found—

A marriage cast on sand

The mirror hideth naught from one so vain,
it masketh not the truth from blinded eyes;
for in thy glass thou findest not thy pain
—to love but of thyself is hate's disguise.
Our union is a marriage cast on sand,
its roots unwatered, built on proud neglect;
thou'st closed thy heart, refusèd to withstand
yet claim to rule, as though my love were debt.
Narcissus is the banner thou dost raise,
no bluster may thy naked truth conceal.
Thro' greed, thou stript my beauty from its blaze
and bled my spirit dry of what was real.
"Our precious, precious union" is thy cry
—yet judgment waits behind the mystic eye.

—to love but of thyself is hate's disguise—

Eternal refrains

When winter whispers of thy poet's rest
with downy sleep that comes to mortal eyes,
which verse of mine, thou mourner, to attest,
shall yet awaken thy heart's loving sighs?
And passing o'er the meter of my rhyme,
wilt thou still find its richness, its desire;
for thee, dear Muse, immortal through all time,
were aye the one to kindle bright its fire.
Not bound by death nor lost to fleeting years,
this ink alone holds memories I shared;
each changing season homage to my fears,
with love imbued, each verse to thee I bared.
Now as my quill lies still, thy heart remains
to weave anew my art in fresh refrains.

—this ink alone holds memories I shared—

afterword

If these sonnets have found a place within you, then their purpose is fulfilled. Though the hand that shaped them may one day fall still, love—in all its seasons—remains unquiet. It endures in ink, in memory, and in the hush between lines.

Thank you for walking this path of feeling and form. May its music linger with you. And may you find, in your own heart, the courage to love, to lose, and to speak again—not as echo, but as answer.

bobby livingston
poet
glasgow, scotland.

attribution

The four sonnets used to introduce the seasonal sections of this collection are by William Shakespeare. These works are in the public domain and have been included with deep respect for their enduring beauty and emotional resonance.

—"*who will believe my verse in time to come*" – *sonnet 17*

—"*summer's lease hath all too short a date*" – *sonnet 18*

—"*for thy sweet love remember'd such wealth brings*" – *sonnet 29*

—"*in black ink my love may still shine bright*" – *sonnet 65*

ISBN: 978-0-9571054-6-1
Typeset & designed by TCA in Glasgow, Scotland.

the year belovèd

sonnets for the seasons of the heart

bobby livingston

www.ingramcontent.com/pod-product-compliance
Lightning Source LLC
LaVergne TN
LVHW051017080826
845145LV00009B/2679